This Workbook Belongs To:

____

If Found Please:

____

This workbook has been designed to help you develop different ways of thinking, behaving, and reacting to situations that cause anxiety. It can also help you learn and practice social skills, which will help you to manage and overcome social anxiety disorder.

This workbook will help you identify and then balance nonsensical thoughts and the underlying anxiety they cause.

The worksheets help you focus on confronting the fears that create anxiety. Helping you to once again be able to engage in activities you may have been avoiding.

Knowledge is power and the more you drill down into your anxiety and begin to really understand it, the more likely you are to live an enjoyable and successful life.

Date _______________________   Source of Anxiety _______________________

Time _______________________   Physical Sensations _______________________

Place _______________________

Negative Beliefs

About Yourself	About Situation

What facts do you know are true?

About Yourself	About Situation

Color where you feel
sensations of anxiety

Is there a more balanced way to think about this situation

What has helped before?   What is helping now?

--- Coping Mechanisms ---

Breathe
Remind yourself that anxiety is just a feeling
Describe your surroundings in detail
Go outdoors
Sip a warm or iced drink slowly
Ground yourself

Date _______________

Time _______________

Place _______________

Source of Anxiety _______________

Physical Sensations _______________

Color where you feel
sensations of anxiety

Negative Beliefs

About Yourself	About Situation

What facts do you know are true?

About Yourself	About Situation

Is there a more balanced way to think about this situation

What has helped before?

What is helping now?

Coping Mechanisms

Breathe
Remind yourself that anxiety is just a feeling
Describe your surroundings in detail
Go outdoors
Sip a warm or iced drink slowly
Ground yourself

Date _________________

Source of Anxiety _________________

Time _________________

Physical Sensations _________________

Place _________________

Negative Beliefs

About Yourself	About Situation

What facts do you know are true?

About Yourself	About Situation

Color where you feel sensations of anxiety

Is there a more balanced way to think about this situation

What has helped before?

What is helping now?

Coping Mechanisms

Breathe
Remind yourself that anxiety is just a feeling
Describe your surroundings in detail
Go outdoors
Sip a warm or iced drink slowly
Ground yourself

Date _______________________   Source of Anxiety _______________________

Time _______________________   Physical Sensations _______________________

Place _______________________

Negative Beliefs

About Yourself	About Situation

What facts do you know are true?

About Yourself	About Situation

Color where you feel
sensations of anxiety

Is there a more balanced way to think about this situation

What has helped before?   What is helping now?

Coping Mechanisms

Breathe
Remind yourself that anxiety is just a feeling
Describe your surroundings in detail
Go outdoors
Sip a warm or iced drink slowly
Ground yourself

Date _______________

Time _______________

Place _______________

Source of Anxiety _______________

Physical Sensations _______________

Negative Beliefs

About Yourself	About Situation

What facts do you know are true?

About Yourself	About Situation

Color where you feel
sensations of anxiety

Is there a more balanced way to think about this situation

What has helped before?

What is helping now?

Coping Mechanisms

Breathe
Remind yourself that anxiety is just a feeling
Describe your surroundings in detail
Go outdoors
Sip a warm or iced drink slowly
Ground yourself

Date _______________________ Source of Anxiety _______________________

Time _______________________ Physical Sensations _______________________

Place _______________________

Negative Beliefs

About Yourself	About Situation

What facts do you know are true?

About Yourself	About Situation

Color where you feel
sensations of anxiety

Is there a more balanced way to think about this situation

What has helped before?

What is helping now?

Coping Mechanisms

Breathe
Remind yourself that anxiety is just a feeling
Describe your surroundings in detail
Go outdoors
Sip a warm or iced drink slowly
Ground yourself

Date _________________________

Time _________________________

Place _________________________

Source of Anxiety _________________________

Physical Sensations _________________________

Negative Beliefs

About Yourself	About Situation

What facts do you know are true?

About Yourself	About Situation

Color where you feel sensations of anxiety

Is there a more balanced way to think about this situation

What has helped before?

What is helping now?

Coping Mechanisms

Breathe
Remind yourself that anxiety is just a feeling
Describe your surroundings in detail
Go outdoors
Sip a warm or iced drink slowly
Ground yourself

Date _________________________   Source of Anxiety _________________________

Time _________________________   Physical Sensations _________________________

Place _________________________

Negative Beliefs

About Yourself	About Situation

What facts do you know are true?

About Yourself	About Situation

Color where you feel
sensations of anxiety

Is there a more balanced way to think about this situation

What has helped before?   What is helping now?

Breathe
Remind yourself that anxiety is just a feeling
Describe your surroundings in detail
Go outdoors
Sip a warm or iced drink slowly
Ground yourself

Date _______________________   Source of Anxiety _______________________

Time _______________________   Physical Sensations _______________________

Place _______________________

Negative Beliefs

About Yourself	About Situation

What facts do you know are true?

About Yourself	About Situation

Color where you feel
sensations of anxiety

Is there a more balanced way to think about this situation

What has helped before?

What is helping now?

Coping Mechanisms

Breathe
Remind yourself that anxiety is just a feeling
Describe your surroundings in detail
Go outdoors
Sip a warm or iced drink slowly
Ground yourself

Date _______________________

Time _______________________

Place _______________________

Source of Anxiety _______________________

Physical Sensations _______________________

Negative Beliefs

About Yourself	About Situation

What facts do you know are true?

About Yourself	About Situation

Color where you feel
sensations of anxiety

Is there a more balanced way to think about this situation

What has helped before?

What is helping now?

Coping Mechanisms

Breathe
Remind yourself that anxiety is just a feeling
Describe your surroundings in detail
Go outdoors
Sip a warm or iced drink slowly
Ground yourself

Date ___________________

Time ___________________

Place ___________________

Source of Anxiety ___________________

Physical Sensations ___________________

Negative Beliefs

About Yourself	About Situation

What facts do you know are true?

About Yourself	About Situation

Color where you feel
sensations of anxiety

Is there a more balanced way to think about this situation

What has helped before?

What is helping now?

Coping Mechanisms

Breathe
Remind yourself that anxiety is just a feeling
Describe your surroundings in detail
Go outdoors
Sip a warm or iced drink slowly
Ground yourself

Date _________________	Source of Anxiety _________________
Time _________________	Physical Sensations _________________
Place _________________	

Negative Beliefs

About Yourself	About Situation

What facts do you know are true?

About Yourself	About Situation

Color where you feel sensations of anxiety

Is there a more balanced way to think about this situation

What has helped before?

What is helping now?

Coping Mechanisms

Breathe
Remind yourself that anxiety is just a feeling
Describe your surroundings in detail
Go outdoors
Sip a warm or iced drink slowly
Ground yourself

Date _______________________

Source of Anxiety _______________________

Time _______________________

Physical Sensations _______________________

Place _______________________

Negative Beliefs

About Yourself	About Situation

What facts do you know are true?

About Yourself	About Situation

Color where you feel sensations of anxiety

Is there a more balanced way to think about this situation

What has helped before?

What is helping now?

Coping Mechanisms

Breathe
Remind yourself that anxiety is just a feeling
Describe your surroundings in detail
Go outdoors
Sip a warm or iced drink slowly
Ground yourself

Date ___________________

Time ___________________

Place ___________________

Source of Anxiety ___________________

Physical Sensations ___________________

Negative Beliefs

About Yourself	About Situation

What facts do you know are true?

About Yourself	About Situation

Color where you feel
sensations of anxiety

Is there a more balanced way to think about this situation

What has helped before?

What is helping now?

Coping Mechanisms

Breathe
Remind yourself that anxiety is just a feeling
Describe your surroundings in detail
Go outdoors
Sip a warm or iced drink slowly
Ground yourself

Date ________________   Source of Anxiety ________________

Time ________________   Physical Sensations ________________

Place ________________

Negative Beliefs

About Yourself	About Situation

What facts do you know are true?

About Yourself	About Situation

Color where you feel
sensations of anxiety

Is there a more balanced way to think about this situation

What has helped before?   What is helping now?

Coping Mechanisms

Breathe
Remind yourself that anxiety is just a feeling
Describe your surroundings in detail
Go outdoors
Sip a warm or iced drink slowly
Ground yourself

Date ___________________

Source of Anxiety ___________________

Time ___________________

Physical Sensations ___________________

Place ___________________

Negative Beliefs

About Yourself	About Situation

What facts do you know are true?

About Yourself	About Situation

Color where you feel sensations of anxiety

Is there a more balanced way to think about this situation

What has helped before?

What is helping now?

Coping Mechanisms

Breathe
Remind yourself that anxiety is just a feeling
Describe your surroundings in detail
Go outdoors
Sip a warm or iced drink slowly
Ground yourself

Date ____ Source of Anxiety ______________________________

Time ____ Physical Sensations ______________________________

Place ____

Negative Beliefs

About Yourself	About Situation

What facts do you know are true?

About Yourself	About Situation

Color where you feel
sensations of anxiety

Is there a more balanced way to think about this situation

What has helped before?

What is helping now?

Coping Mechanisms

Breathe
Remind yourself that anxiety is just a feeling
Describe your surroundings in detail
Go outdoors
Sip a warm or iced drink slowly
Ground yourself

Date _________________

Source of Anxiety _________________

Time _________________

Physical Sensations _________________

Place _________________

Negative Beliefs

About Yourself	About Situation

What facts do you know are true?

About Yourself	About Situation

Color where you feel
sensations of anxiety

Is there a more balanced way to think about this situation

What has helped before?

What is helping now?

Coping Mechanisms

Breathe
Remind yourself that anxiety is just a feeling
Describe your surroundings in detail
Go outdoors
Sip a warm or iced drink slowly
Ground yourself

Date _______________   Source of Anxiety _______________

Time _______________   Physical Sensations _______________

Place _______________

Negative Beliefs

About Yourself	About Situation

What facts do you know are true?

About Yourself	About Situation

Color where you feel
sensations of anxiety

Is there a more balanced way to think about this situation

What has helped before?   What is helping now?

Coping Mechanisms

Breathe
Remind yourself that anxiety is just a feeling
Describe your surroundings in detail
Go outdoors
Sip a warm or iced drink slowly
Ground yourself

Date ______________________

Time ______________________

Place ______________________

Source of Anxiety ______________________

Physical Sensations ______________________

Negative Beliefs

About Yourself	About Situation

What facts do you know are true?

About Yourself	About Situation

Color where you feel
sensations of anxiety

Is there a more balanced way to think about this situation

What has helped before?

What is helping now?

Coping Mechanisms

Breathe
Remind yourself that anxiety is just a feeling
Describe your surroundings in detail
Go outdoors
Sip a warm or iced drink slowly
Ground yourself

Date _______________________

Source of Anxiety _______________________

Time _______________________

Physical Sensations _______________________

Place _______________________

Negative Beliefs

About Yourself	About Situation

What facts do you know are true?

About Yourself	About Situation

Is there a more balanced way to think about this situation

What has helped before?

What is helping now?

Coping Mechanisms

Breathe
Remind yourself that anxiety is just a feeling
Describe your surroundings in detail
Go outdoors
Sip a warm or iced drink slowly
Ground yourself

Date ____________________

Time ____________________

Place ____________________

Source of Anxiety ____________________

Physical Sensations ____________________

Negative Beliefs

About Yourself	About Situation

What facts do you know are true?

About Yourself	About Situation

Color where you feel
sensations of anxiety

Is there a more balanced way to think about this situation

What has helped before?

What is helping now?

Coping Mechanisms

Breathe
Remind yourself that anxiety is just a feeling
Describe your surroundings in detail
Go outdoors
Sip a warm or iced drink slowly
Ground yourself

Date _______________

Source of Anxiety _______________

Time _______________

Physical Sensations _______________

Place _______________

Negative Beliefs

About Yourself	About Situation

What facts do you know are true?

About Yourself	About Situation

Color where you feel
sensations of anxiety

Is there a more balanced way to think about this situation

What has helped before?

What is helping now?

Coping Mechanisms

Breathe
Remind yourself that anxiety is just a feeling
Describe your surroundings in detail
Go outdoors
Sip a warm or iced drink slowly
Ground yourself

Date ___________________

Time ___________________

Place ___________________

Source of Anxiety ___________________

Physical Sensations ___________________

Negative Beliefs

About Yourself	About Situation

What facts do you know are true?

About Yourself	About Situation

Color where you feel sensations of anxiety

Is there a more balanced way to think about this situation

What has helped before?

What is helping now?

Coping Mechanisms

Breathe
Remind yourself that anxiety is just a feeling
Describe your surroundings in detail
Go outdoors
Sip a warm or iced drink slowly
Ground yourself

Date _______________________   Source of Anxiety _______________________

Time _______________________   Physical Sensations _______________________

Place _______________________

Negative Beliefs

About Yourself	About Situation

What facts do you know are true?

About Yourself	About Situation

Is there a more balanced way to think about this situation

What has helped before?

What is helping now?

Coping Mechanisms

Breathe
Remind yourself that anxiety is just a feeling
Describe your surroundings in detail
Go outdoors
Sip a warm or iced drink slowly
Ground yourself

Date ____________________   Source of Anxiety ____________________

Time ____________________   Physical Sensations ____________________

Place ____________________

Negative Beliefs

About Yourself	About Situation

What facts do you know are true?

About Yourself	About Situation

Color where you feel sensations of anxiety

Is there a more balanced way to think about this situation

What has helped before?   What is helping now?

Coping Mechanisms

Breathe
Remind yourself that anxiety is just a feeling
Describe your surroundings in detail
Go outdoors
Sip a warm or iced drink slowly
Ground yourself

Date _______________   Source of Anxiety _______________

Time _______________   Physical Sensations _______________

Place _______________

Negative Beliefs

About Yourself	About Situation

What facts do you know are true?

About Yourself	About Situation

Color where you feel
sensations of anxiety

Is there a more balanced way to think about this situation

What has helped before?   What is helping now?

Coping Mechanisms

Breathe
Remind yourself that anxiety is just a feeling
Describe your surroundings in detail
Go outdoors
Sip a warm or iced drink slowly
Ground yourself

Date _________________

Time _________________

Place _________________

Source of Anxiety _________________

Physical Sensations _________________

Negative Beliefs

About Yourself	About Situation

What facts do you know are true?

About Yourself	About Situation

Color where you feel
sensations of anxiety

Is there a more balanced way to think about this situation

What has helped before?

What is helping now?

Coping Mechanisms

Breathe
Remind yourself that anxiety is just a feeling
Describe your surroundings in detail
Go outdoors
Sip a warm or iced drink slowly
Ground yourself

Date _______________   Source of Anxiety _______________

Time _______________   Physical Sensations _______________

Place _______________

Negative Beliefs

About Yourself	About Situation

What facts do you know are true?

About Yourself	About Situation

Color where you feel
sensations of anxiety

Is there a more balanced way to think about this situation

What has helped before?   What is helping now?

Coping Mechanisms

Breathe
Remind yourself that anxiety is just a feeling
Describe your surroundings in detail
Go outdoors
Sip a warm or iced drink slowly
Ground yourself

Date _______________   Source of Anxiety _______________

Time _______________   Physical Sensations _______________

Place _______________

Negative Beliefs

About Yourself	About Situation

What facts do you know are true?

About Yourself	About Situation

Color where you feel
sensations of anxiety

Is there a more balanced way to think about this situation

What has helped before?   What is helping now?

Coping Mechanisms

Breathe
Remind yourself that anxiety is just a feeling
Describe your surroundings in detail
Go outdoors
Sip a warm or iced drink slowly
Ground yourself

Date _______________________   Source of Anxiety _______________________

Time _______________________   Physical Sensations _______________________

Place _______________________

Negative Beliefs

About Yourself	About Situation

What facts do you know are true?

About Yourself	About Situation

Color where you feel
sensations of anxiety

Is there a more balanced way to think about this situation

What has helped before?   What is helping now?

Coping Mechanisms

Breathe
Remind yourself that anxiety is just a feeling
Describe your surroundings in detail
Go outdoors
Sip a warm or iced drink slowly
Ground yourself

Date ___________________   Source of Anxiety ___________________

Time ___________________   Physical Sensations ___________________

Place ___________________

Negative Beliefs

About Yourself	About Situation

What facts do you know are true?

About Yourself	About Situation

Color where you feel
sensations of anxiety

Is there a more balanced way to think about this situation

What has helped before?

What is helping now?

Coping Mechanisms

Breathe
Remind yourself that anxiety is just a feeling
Describe your surroundings in detail
Go outdoors
Sip a warm or iced drink slowly
Ground yourself

Date ______________________

Time ______________________

Place ______________________

Source of Anxiety ______________________

Physical Sensations ______________________

Negative Beliefs

About Yourself	About Situation

What facts do you know are true?

About Yourself	About Situation

Color where you feel
sensations of anxiety

Is there a more balanced way to think about this situation

What has helped before?

What is helping now?

Coping Mechanisms

Breathe
Remind yourself that anxiety is just a feeling
Describe your surroundings in detail
Go outdoors
Sip a warm or iced drink slowly
Ground yourself

Date _______________

Source of Anxiety _______________

Time _______________

Physical Sensations _______________

Place _______________

Negative Beliefs

About Yourself	About Situation

What facts do you know are true?

About Yourself	About Situation

Color where you feel sensations of anxiety

Is there a more balanced way to think about this situation

What has helped before?

What is helping now?

Coping Mechanisms

Breathe
Remind yourself that anxiety is just a feeling
Describe your surroundings in detail
Go outdoors
Sip a warm or iced drink slowly
Ground yourself

Date ______________________   Source of Anxiety ______________________

Time ______________________   Physical Sensations ______________________

Place ______________________

Negative Beliefs

About Yourself	About Situation

What facts do you know are true?

About Yourself	About Situation

Color where you feel
sensations of anxiety

Is there a more balanced way to think about this situation

What has helped before?   What is helping now?

Coping Mechanisms

Breathe
Remind yourself that anxiety is just a feeling
Describe your surroundings in detail
Go outdoors
Sip a warm or iced drink slowly
Ground yourself

Date ________________

Source of Anxiety ________________

Time ________________

Physical Sensations ________________

Place ________________

Negative Beliefs

About Yourself	About Situation

What facts do you know are true?

About Yourself	About Situation

Color where you feel
sensations of anxiety

Is there a more balanced way to think about this situation

What has helped before?

What is helping now?

Coping Mechanisms

Breathe
Remind yourself that anxiety is just a feeling
Describe your surroundings in detail
Go outdoors
Sip a warm or iced drink slowly
Ground yourself

Date ______________________

Source of Anxiety ______________________

Time ______________________

Physical Sensations ______________________

Place ______________________

Negative Beliefs

About Yourself	About Situation

What facts do you know are true?

About Yourself	About Situation

Color where you feel sensations of anxiety

Is there a more balanced way to think about this situation

What has helped before?

What is helping now?

Coping Mechanisms

Breathe
Remind yourself that anxiety is just a feeling
Describe your surroundings in detail
Go outdoors
Sip a warm or iced drink slowly
Ground yourself

Date ______________________

Source of Anxiety ______________________

Time ______________________

Physical Sensations ______________________

Place ______________________

Negative Beliefs

About Yourself	About Situation

What facts do you know are true?

About Yourself	About Situation

Color where you feel
sensations of anxiety

Is there a more balanced way to think about this situation

What has helped before?

What is helping now?

Coping Mechanisms

Breathe
Remind yourself that anxiety is just a feeling
Describe your surroundings in detail
Go outdoors
Sip a warm or iced drink slowly
Ground yourself

Date

Time

Place

Source of Anxiety

Physical Sensations

Negative Beliefs

About Yourself	About Situation

What facts do you know are true?

About Yourself	About Situation

Color where you feel
sensations of anxiety

Is there a more balanced way to think about this situation

What has helped before?

What is helping now?

Coping Mechanisms

Breathe
Remind yourself that anxiety is just a feeling
Describe your surroundings in detail
Go outdoors
Sip a warm or iced drink slowly
Ground yourself

Date ________________	Source of Anxiety ________________
Time ________________	Physical Sensations ________________
Place ________________	

Negative Beliefs

About Yourself	About Situation

What facts do you know are true?

About Yourself	About Situation

Color where you feel
sensations of anxiety

Is there a more balanced way to think about this situation

What has helped before?

What is helping now?

Coping Mechanisms

Breathe
Remind yourself that anxiety is just a feeling
Describe your surroundings in detail
Go outdoors
Sip a warm or iced drink slowly
Ground yourself

Date ______________________

Source of Anxiety ______________________

Time ______________________

Physical Sensations ______________________

Place ______________________

Negative Beliefs

About Yourself	About Situation

What facts do you know are true?

About Yourself	About Situation

Color where you feel sensations of anxiety

Is there a more balanced way to think about this situation

What has helped before?

What is helping now?

Coping Mechanisms

Breathe
Remind yourself that anxiety is just a feeling
Describe your surroundings in detail
Go outdoors
Sip a warm or iced drink slowly
Ground yourself

Date _______________________

Time _______________________

Place _______________________

Source of Anxiety _______________________

Physical Sensations _______________________

Negative Beliefs

About Yourself	About Situation

What facts do you know are true?

About Yourself	About Situation

Color where you feel sensations of anxiety

Is there a more balanced way to think about this situation

What has helped before?

What is helping now?

Coping Mechanisms

Breathe
Remind yourself that anxiety is just a feeling
Describe your surroundings in detail
Go outdoors
Sip a warm or iced drink slowly
Ground yourself

Date _______________

Source of Anxiety _______________

Time _______________

Physical Sensations _______________

Place _______________

Negative Beliefs

About Yourself	About Situation

What facts do you know are true?

About Yourself	About Situation

Color where you feel sensations of anxiety

Is there a more balanced way to think about this situation

What has helped before?

What is helping now?

Coping Mechanisms

Breathe
Remind yourself that anxiety is just a feeling
Describe your surroundings in detail
Go outdoors
Sip a warm or iced drink slowly
Ground yourself